WonderWorks

Decodable Reader

Unit 8

Mc Graw Hill

Contents

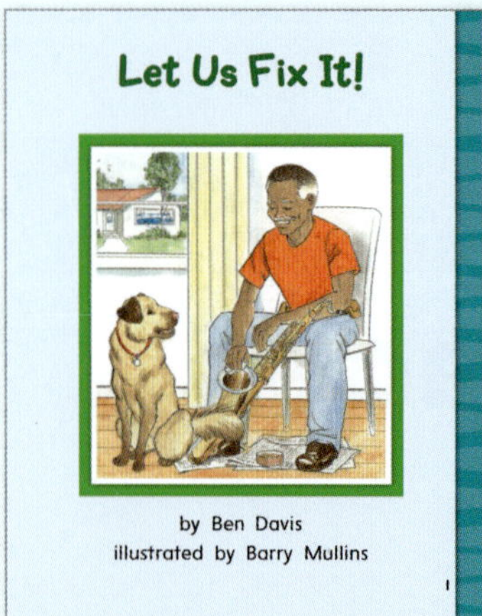
Let Us Fix It!
by Ben Davis
illustrated by Barry Mullins
1

At My Job
by Lily Higgins
9

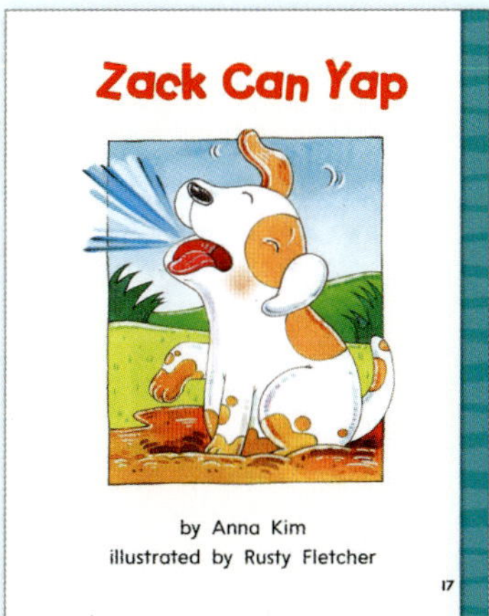
Zack Can Yap
by Anna Kim
illustrated by Rusty Fletcher
17

Let Us Fix It!

by Ben Davis
illustrated by Barry Mullins

Vin had a big dog, Max.
Big Max was six.

"**Want** to fix it, Big Max?"
Vin and Big Max fix the box.

Vin had a big sax.
Big Max got wax.
"Let us wax it," **said** Vin.

Vin had a fat red fox.
It had a big rip in it.
Vin and Big Max fix it up.

Vin got a big pad.
Big Max got a red pen.

They fix a box, sax, and fox.

At My Job

Digital Vision/PunchStock

by Lily Higgins

Ingolf Pompe 35/Alamy

Alex Segre/Alamy

Ted can get gas.
The red cab is quick.

Ingolf Pompe 35/Alamy

Meg is up on deck.
It can get wet on the job.

Digital Vision/PunchStock

Jan can get in a big jet.
Jan can go up, up, up.

Peter Grumann/The Image Bank/Getty Images

Jim can jog and kick.
Jim can not quit.
Jim can kick it in!

Stockbroker/SuperStock

Pam can fix a big jam.
Tap, tap, tap!
Pam can fix it up.

(tl) Stockbroker/SuperStock; (tr) Alex Segre/Alamy; (c) Ingolf Pompe 35/Alamy; (bl) Peter Grumann/The Image Bank/Getty Images; (br): Digital Vision/PunchStock

Here is my job.
Can you see **me**?

Zack Can Yap

by Anna Kim

illustrated by Rusty Fletcher

This is Zack in mud.
Zack can not get up.
Zack can yap, yap yap.

Val and Kim zip up in a van.
Kim said, "Zack is here.
We can pick him up."

"Hop in the van," said Val.
Zack can not get in yet.

Zack can not get up.
Zack is sad.
What can Zack do?

Val and Kim hop in mud.
They pet Zack.
Zack did not yap.

Yes! Zack is not in mud.
Zack got in the van.

Steve's Huge Step

by Akisha Owens
illustrated by Meryl Henderson

Steve has tunes at his home. Steve likes **old** and new tunes. Steve hopes to get in the band.

Steve totes a case
to class.
Steve waves at Mom.
Mom waves back.

Steve chose a cute tune
from long **ago**.
He sits at his stand.
Steve hits all his notes.

This **boy** and **girl** check on **how** to play notes. It is a long song. They can not make a mistake.

These kids hope to get in the band too.

People who are judges will pick the kids.

Steve made it in the band! It is a huge step. Steve closes his case. It is time to get home and tell Mom.

Unit 3

Word Count: 101

Decodable Words

Target Phonics Elements: Consonant Digraphs *ch, -tch, ph*
checks, chicks, ditch, fetch, hitch, inch, Mitch, Mitch's, munch, Phil, ranch
Review: *a, and, at, best, big, bring, Dad, Dad's, did, has, helps, his, in, is, it, must, not, peck, pen, snack, stuck, them, this, truck, tugs, van, will*

High-Frequency Words

around, by, many, place, walk
Review: *go, likes, look, moves, out, the, to*

Word Count: 127

Decodable Words

Target Phonics Element: Long *a (a_e)*
escape, make, safe, same, scales, shake, snake, snakes
Review: *a, and, act, as, blend, can, can't, dead, den, dig, end, fast, flop, get, help, huff, hiss, if, in, is, it, it's, its land, legs, logs, nest, nests, not, on, plants, rock, sand, slip, spot, spotted, then, this, will, wings*

High-Frequency Words

away, now, some, today, way, why
Review: *be, does, have, look, move, one, they, to, too, under, what*

Week 5 • *Steve's Huge Step* .... page 33

Word Count: 115

Decodable Words

Target Phonics Elements: Long *o (o_e)*, Long *u (u_e)*, Long *e (e_e)*

chose, closes, cute, home, hope, hopes, huge, notes, totes, tune, tunes, Steve, Steve's

Review: *a, and, at, back, band, can, case, checks, class, get, has, his, hits, in, is, it, judges, kids, likes, long, made, make, mistake, Mom, not, on, pick, sits, song, stand, step, tell, this, time, waves, will*

High-Frequency Words

ago, boy, girl, how, old, people

Review: *all, are, from, he, new, play, the, these, they, to, too, who*

Decoding skills taught to date:

Phonics: Short *a*; Short *i*; l-Blends; Short *o*; *r*-Blends, *s*-Blends; Short *e (e, ea)*; Short u; End Blends *nd, nk, nt, st, sk, mp;* Consonant Digraphs: *th, sh, -ng*; Consonant Digraphs *ch, -tch, wh, ph;* Long *a (a_e);* Long *i (i_e);* Soft *c;* Soft *g, dge;* Long *o (o_e);* Long *u (u_e);* Long *e (e_e)*

Structural Analysis: Inflectional Ending *-s* (plurals, verbs); Double Final Consonants; Alphabetical Order; Possessives with *'s;* Inflectional Ending *-ed;* Contractions with *'s;* Inflectional Ending *-ing;* Closed Syllables; Inflectional Ending *-es;* Contractions with n*'t;* Plurals with CVC*e* Words; Inflectional Endings *-ed, -ing* with Spelling Changes; CVC*e* Syllables

Decoding skills taught to date:

Consonants /m/*m*, /s/*s*, /p/*p*, /t/*t;* Short *a;* Short *i;* Initial and Final /n/*n;* Initial /k/*c;* Short *o;* Initial and Final /d/*d;* Consonant /h/*h;* Short *e;* Blends *sn, sp, st;* Consonants /f/*f*, /r/*r;* Initial and Final /b/*b;* Consonant /l/*l;* Initial /k/*k;* Digraph *ck;* Short *u;* Initial and Final /g/*g;* Consonant /w/*w;* Consonants /ks/*x*, /v/*v;* Consonants /j/*j*, /qu/*qu;* Consonants /y/*y*, /z/*z*

Week 3 • *Zack Can Yap*

Word Count: 85

Decodable Words

Target Phonics Elements: Consonants */y/y, /z/z*
yap, yes, yet, Zack, zip
Review: *can, did, get, got, him, hop, in, Kim, mud, not, pet, pick, sad, up, Val, van*

High-Frequency Words

this, what
Review: *a, and, do, here, is, said, the, they, we*

Unit 8

Word Count: 80

Decodable Words

Target Phonics Elements: Consonants /ks/*x*, /v/*v*
box, fix, fox, Max, sax, six, Vin, wax
Review: *big, dog, fat, got, had, in, it, let, pad, pen, red, rip, up, us*

High-Frequency Words

said, want
Review: *a, and, they, to, was*

Word Count: 73

Decodable Words

Target Phonics Element: Consonants /j/*j*, /qu/*qu*
jam, Jan, jet, Jim, job, jog, quick, quit
Review: *at, big, cab, can, deck, fix, gas, get, in, it, kick, Meg, on, Pam, red, tap, Ted, up, wet*

High-Frequency Words

here, me
Review: *a, and, go, is, my, see, the, you*